America's Urban Parks

by Thomas Pressel

 HOUGHTON MIFFLIN HARCOURT

PHOTOGRAPHY CREDITS: **Cover** © Helene Rogers/Alamy. **Title page** © David Sanger Photography/Alamy. **4** © Bruce Heinemann/Photodisc/Getty Images. **5** Jo-Ann Ordano © California Academy of Sciences. **6** © Darryl Bush/San Francisco Chronicle/CORBIS. **7** © john t. fowler/Alamy **8** © David Sanger Photography/Alamy. **10** © Ron Chapple Stock/Alamy. **11** © Manfred Danegger/zefa/CORBIS. **18** © Helene Rogers/Alamy.

All other photos © Houghton Mifflin Harcourt Publishers

Printed in China

ISBN: 978-0-547-89068-5

10 11 12 13 14 15 0940 21 20 19 18 17 16

4500569761   A B C D E F G

Table of Contents

Introduction to America's Urban Parks

When you hear the word *park*, what comes to mind? You may think of popular national parks such as Yellowstone or Yosemite. You may picture small patches of green among tall buildings in a large city. But do you picture miles of open space in the middle of big cities? You should. Some of America's most beautiful parks are found in our largest cities.

This book explores America's urban parks. An urban park is one that exists in or beside a busy, modern city. Urban parks have many purposes:

- They provide relief from the stress of city life.
- They offer opportunities for recreation and exercise.
- Some urban parks protect endangered species that live within their boundaries.
- Many urban parks preserve the history and culture of the community.

The people who manage America's urban parks are the guardians of many important sites. They try hard to keep human activity from harming our parks. This is a difficult task. Traffic, pollution, and careless visitors can harm the plants and animals in urban parks. As visitors, it is our responsibility to respect the wildlife in them.

Some urban parks are part of our National Park System. Others are run by local city governments. Large or small, old or new, urban parks are here for all of us to enjoy.

San Francisco's Presidio

Here Today... Imagine that you are hiking in an urban park. You look down and see an unusual plant. It's not like any plant you have ever seen. You observe it carefully and snap a picture. Later, you take the photo to the ranger station.

When the park ranger sees it, she gives a low whistle. She tells you that the plant you saw is called Raven's manzanita. It is very rare, and it is endangered. But that's not all. The particular plant you saw is the last wild Raven's manzanita on Earth.

Gone Tomorrow? The last wild Raven's manzanita clings to a windy slope facing the Pacific Ocean. This hillside is part of the San Francisco Presidio, one of the nation's newest national parks. The Presidio is an urban park. Just outside the Presidio gates, taxis zoom down crowded streets. Radios blare from car stereos. Cell phones ring. Raven's manzanita is a small, quiet reminder of the great variety of wild plants that once grew here.

Wildflowers bloom in an urban park.

The last existing Raven's manzanita shrub was discovered in the 1950s by a teenager, Peter Raven. The plant was named after him.

Even before San Francisco was built, there were only a few wild places where Raven's manzanita could survive. That's because the plant needs a unique set of conditions. It needs soil made from serpentine, California's state rock. Serpentine rock is greenish-gray, smooth, and scaly—like a serpent's skin. It came from deep below Earth's surface. Millions of years ago, it was pushed upward to the surface when Earth's plates moved.

Soil made of serpentine sand covers parts of the Presidio. Serpentine soil is low in nutrients and contains some toxic metals, so not many plants can grow in it. Raven's manzanita is one of the few plants that has adapted to serpentine soil. This is the only kind of soil it can live in. Unless the Raven's manzanita's habitat is protected, this rare plant will disappear from the wild forever.

Shaping Nature The photograph below shows part of the Presidio now. In 1776, when Spanish explorers arrived there, it looked very different. There were no forests at all. Instead, the land was a series of windswept hills with short, scrubby vegetation. The Spanish built a fort, which they named *Presidio de San Francisco*. They constructed buildings of adobe (mud bricks).

The U.S. Army took control of the Presidio in 1846. Its location on San Francisco Bay made the Presidio valuable as a military base. However, the treeless, windswept landscape seemed cold and unattractive to army officials. Winds from the Pacific Ocean caused the sand dunes to shift constantly. Blowing sand often filled the air. The army planted thousands of trees to solve these problems. Today, forests of eucalyptus and other trees cover a lot of the Presidio. The wind is calmer inside these forests and in the areas they shelter.

The Presidio today

The Short Road to Extinction The U.S. Army wasn't thinking about how the new forest would affect the wildlife in the Presidio. The trees had a negative effect on many of the area's native plants and animals. Native plants and animals are those that live in a place naturally, without having been brought there by humans. When nonnative plants or animals are introduced into an area, they can crowd out native life that is already there. Blue gum eucalyptus and Monterey cypress are two types of nonnative trees the army planted in the Presidio. They grew very well there. However, they took more than their share of sunlight and water. They crowded out many of the native shrubs and wildflowers.

When plants in an area change or die, animals that depend on them must adapt, find another place to live, or die. Such was the case of the Xerces Blue butterfly. It once lived on certain slopes of the Presidio. As the butterfly's habitat changed, its

Xerces Blue butterfly

population decreased. Sadly, the last Xerces Blue was seen fluttering over the sand dunes in 1942. This was the first recorded butterfly extinction in North America.

Restoring Native Habitats Today's Presidio may seem like a natural place, but it's not the natural place that once existed. It has been shaped by humans to meet human needs. Many people believe that the Presidio's rare serpentine soils and windswept dunes are worth preserving. They argue that not only are these natural areas unique, they also support rare life forms, such as Raven's manzanita. The National Park Service has been trying to restore several sites in the park to their native state. They hope that by doing this, they will help the region's unique plants and animals to survive.

When the Presidio was an army base, part of its land was used as a dumping site for military waste. Gas and oil leaked into the ground. The National Park Service has worked hard to restore these areas. They have removed toxic soil and planted native shrubs and grasses.

Crissy Field used to be an airfield. Part of it has been turned into a tidal marsh. Native plants grow in the sand dunes nearby.

Rock Creek Park, Washington, D.C.

Crustaceans in the Capital Now imagine that you are visiting another urban park—Rock Creek National Park in Washington, D.C. You are part of a 24-hour wildlife-counting survey. (A survey is a careful study and report.) During the survey, hundreds of volunteers work with park officials. Their job is to find and record wildlife. Every insect, fish, bird, and animal in sight will be counted. The survey will help park officials see how animal populations have changed.

You are working along a small stream, searching for animals that live in it. Your group has found a cluster of tiny shrimplike creatures. The animals are colorless and blind. Each one is just 10 millimeters long—the length of a staple. You have found examples of Hay's spring amphipod. It is a crustacean, like shrimp and crab.

Your amphipod discovery is a good one. This particular creature is found only in Rock Creek National Park. Five small streams within the park are the last places on Earth where these animals still live.

Amphipods are sensitive to water quality. This amphipod can exist only because the park protects its water from pollutants such as fertilizer and oil products.

About Rock Creek National Park Founded in 1890, Rock Creek is one of the nation's largest urban parks. Unlike the Presidio, where nature was shaped by humans, Rock Creek is a natural habitat. Park visitors may glimpse red foxes, white-tailed deer, and up to 160 kinds of birds.

As at the Presidio, urban activities affect the plants and animals that live in Rock Creek National Park. Some people drive their cars through the park. The traffic adds noise and pollution to the air. Each year, more than 100 animals are killed on roads in or near the park. Although the park service regulates where visitors can go and what they can do, damage does occur. Too many visitors may disturb the animals. Plants suffer when people wander off the trails and trample them.

Rock Creek Park is located near the National Mall.

Accidental Habitats Imagine you are visiting the Lincoln Memorial in Washington, D.C. The parking lot is jam-packed with tour buses. Tourists get off the buses, eager to see the famous statue of Abraham Lincoln.

As you stand in line, you glance the other way—toward a green area to one side of the monument. Movement behind a tree has attracted your gaze. Then you spy a long, pointy nose and two big ears. Is it a dog? No—it's a wild red fox! A red fox in a national park isn't strange. But seeing one at a crowded tourist spot is strange indeed. How did this fox get there? Many urban parklands are connected to other green areas outside their boundaries. Rivers and streams, smaller city parks, and even backyards often create an extended "greenway."

Like squares in a quilt, these connected zones form a natural corridor for animals. A hungry red fox doesn't pay attention to road signs. It just follows its nose. It may follow a greenway for many miles, slipping under fences, jumping over hedges, and running across backyards in search of food. That's how a red fox ended up at the Lincoln Memorial.

Red fox

Preserving Culture

The Layers of the Past Conserving natural habitats is just one role of our urban national parks. National parks like the Presidio and Rock Creek have another important role, as well. They also preserve our history.

Think of history as a set of layers, one on top of another. The top layer—everything you see around you—is the present. Beneath your feet are many other layers. These are the layers of the past.

Once you start digging into these layers, you reveal entire worlds that existed before your time. You find artifacts, or objects people used long ago. Artifacts include pieces of pottery, old forks, toys, bones, and even the contents of garbage dumps. Artifacts tell the story of the different groups of people who have lived in a place. Without careful digging, preservation, and study, these stories would be lost forever.

Arrowheads such as these are artifacts that tell about life long ago.

Layers of Time in the Presidio For over ten thousand years, the Ohlone Indians lived in the area where San Francisco is now. In the late 1700s, Spanish soldiers built the fort there that is now known as the Presidio. They lived inside the walls of the fort in adobe buildings. When California became part of Mexico, Mexican soldiers occupied the Presidio. By that time, most of the old adobe buildings were in ruins.

When the U.S. Army took control of the Presidio in 1846, it started repairing some buildings and constructing new ones. By the time the Presidio became a national park, very little of the Spanish *Presidio* remained. People weren't even sure where its original boundaries were.

In 1993, when the army was getting ready to leave the Presidio, workers made a surprising discovery. They unearthed a row of sturdy stones. Archaeologists were called in. A very large structure had once existed in this location—but what was it?

Workers uncovered more and more stones. They followed the path of buried rock for 500 feet. Archaeologists realized that the foundation of the original *Presidio* had been rediscovered!

The last remaining adobe building in the Presidio is the Officer's Club. It was originally built of adobe, but over time its walls were repaired with other building materials. By 1847, the adobe walls were completely covered by wood.

One archaeologist describes the Officer's Club as a "layer cake." Its core is made of original adobe, stone, and clay. Layer after layer of wood, plaster, and other materials have been added. Now archaeologists are working to uncover parts of the original walls. Their work will give modern visitors a fascinating look at the Presidio's layers of time.

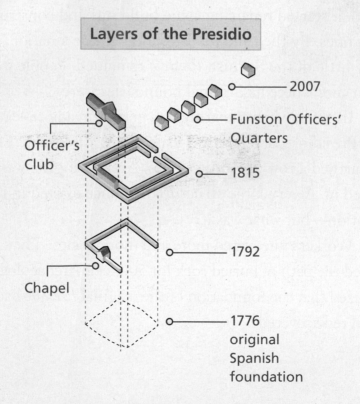

Layers of the Presidio

- 2007
- Funston Officers' Quarters
- Officer's Club
- 1815
- 1792
- Chapel
- 1776 original Spanish foundation

Layers of Time in Rock Creek National Park People have lived near Rock Creek for more than 13,000 years. This was long before anyone started keeping track of history. In more than 10 places in Rock Creek National Park, scientists have discovered the remains of ancient camping sites. They belonged to early Native Americans. Some camps may have been used for thousands of years.

Archaeologists discovered an ancient quarry, as well. A quarry is a place where stone has been cut from a natural deposit of rock. This discovery showed that ancient Native Americans made stone tools. Europeans arrived and began to settle in the region in the mid-1600s. They left their clues behind, too. The diagram on this page shows some of the groups that lived near Rock Creek in the past.

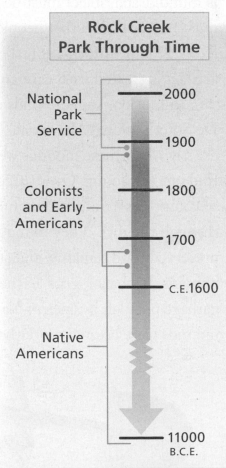

Rock Creek
Park Through Time

National Park Service — 2000

— 1900

Colonists and Early Americans — 1800

— 1700

— C.E. 1600

Native Americans

— 11000 B.C.E.

You Dig!

Have you ever dreamed of finding buried treasure? In some urban parks, people have the chance to work alongside experts who are digging up treasures from the past.

Volunteers who live near Alexandria, Virginia, work with the Alexandria Archaeology Museum to dig artifacts out of the ground. The work doesn't stop when an artifact is found. Each object must be carefully cleaned. Then it must be marked so that people will know where it came from. Finally, information about it must be recorded. Each artifact is treated with care and respect.

In Florida, large mounds called shell ridges lie in the De Soto National Memorial. Archaeologists didn't know exactly when these mounds were created. The only way to find out was to dig. Over three weeks in 1997, hundreds of volunteers carefully dug into the mounds and sifted through the dirt. They found seashells, pottery, tools, preserved food remains, and stones shaped by prehistoric humans. Archaeologists learned that the mounds were garbage piles left by ancient Native Americans. The earliest mounds were created more than 2,000 years ago.

Other Urban Artifacts

When construction begins on new roads, buildings, and houses, digging is often the first step. Sometimes construction workers start digging and find things they never expected to find. Many amazing archaeological sites have been discovered this way. Most cities have laws that allow experts to take a close look at construction sites before construction begins.

Seattle, Washington, has this kind of law. In 2005, the city of Seattle hired archaeologists to look at the future site of a bridge. To everyone's surprise, the archaeologists discovered more than 900 Native American artifacts by digging in just a few places. The site was probably a Native American gathering place that burned down and was forgotten.

In 1991, construction started for an office building in New York City. Soon the project was halted. The workers had discovered an African burial ground from the 1600s and 1700s. Many people believed that the site should not be built on. They persuaded the city of New York to preserve the site. Now the site has been made into a memorial. It is called the African Burial Ground National Monument.

America's Park Architect

Imagine yourself standing at one end of the Back Bay Fens, a beautiful city park in Boston, Massachusetts. You feel like taking a long walk. After two hours, you've covered five miles and six city parks. The parks are connected like bright green jewels on a necklace, strung from one end of the city to the other. This is Boston's "Emerald Necklace."

Boston's Emerald Necklace was created by Frederick Law Olmsted, one of America's first park architects. In his lifetime, Olmsted had a hand in creating more than 500 parks. In 1893, he designed the Linear Park in Atlanta, Georgia, a beautiful chain of parklands. He also designed Central Park in New York City and South Park in Chicago. Olmsted was the first architect to see the importance of urban greenways.

"We want a ground… where [people] may stroll for an hour, seeing, hearing, feeling nothing of the bustle and jar of the streets…"
—Frederick Law Olmsted

Responding

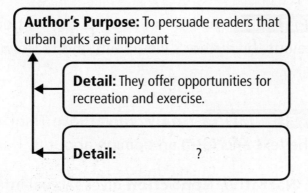 **TARGET SKILL** **Author's Purpose** What was the author's purpose for writing *America's Urban Parks*? Copy the chart below. Summarize the author's purpose. Then list details that support that purpose.

Author's Purpose: To persuade readers that urban parks are important

Detail: They offer opportunities for recreation and exercise.

Detail: ?

Write About It

Text to Text Think of another selection you have read that tells about an environmental issue you support. Write several paragraphs explaining why that issue is important.

adapted	regulate
attracted	responsibility
conserving	restore
endangered	unique
guardians	vegetation

✔ **TARGET SKILL** **Author's Purpose** Use text details to figure out the author's viewpoint and reasons for writing.

✔ **TARGET STRATEGY** **Analyze/Evaluate** Think carefully about the text and form an opinion about it.

GENRE **Narrative Nonfiction** gives factual information by telling a true story.